THIS BOOK is to
commemorate the issuance of the
Papago medal
and in memoriam to Thomas A. Segundo
November 15, 1972
and is limited to 15,000 copies
No.   **LIBRARY**

Western Ways Photograph by Charles W. Herber

PAPAGO WOMAN HARVESTING ripe cactus fruit with wooden "ribs" from saguaro o'
giant cactus.

THE

PAPAGO

PEOPLE

by Henry F. Dobyns

Scientific Editors: Henry F. Dobyns and Robert C. Euler
General Editor: John I. Griffin

PUBLISHED BY INDIAN TRIBAL SERIES / PHOENIX

This volume benefitted from the editorial assistance of Dr. Bernard L. Fontana of the Arizona State Museum.

Library of Congress Catalog Number 72-96750

PRINTED IN THE UNITED STATES OF AMERICA — Imperial Lithographers

ʋGUSTINE LOPEZ Tribal Chairman of the Papago Nation.

IN MEMORIAM

THOMAS A. SEGUNDO

This Book is dedicated to the memory of
Thomas A. Segundo
Chairman
Papago Tribal Council
1947 – 1953
1968 – 1971

"DRINK ONLY A LITTLE WATER!"
This is the kind of admonition Papago fathers used to whisper to their sons and daughters to awaken them in the morning. To the young girls, the message carried peculiar poignancy, because they were the ones who rose before dawn to run to the mountain springs with two small earthen water jars to fill with precious liquid to carefully carry back home to last the entire family all day. Although the girls carried their water jars on their backs in skillfully woven net-and-pole packframes they called *kihau,* the burdens were heavy and the girls had to be careful not to spill the water out of their jars.

The Papago people prided themselves on their thirst-endurance, and well they might, for they inhabited one of the most arid regions in North America. They occupied the semi-arid moun-

1

tains and alluvial valleys sparsely covered by thorny scrub plants forming part of what is now termed the Sonoran Desert, one of four major deserts in North America. The Papagos lived in that portion of the Sonoran Desert located east of the head of the Gulf of California and delta of the Colorado River to the borders of the Santa Cruz River, a permanent stream that arises in southern Arizona, flows into northern Sonora, Mexico, and turns back to the north to empty into the Gila River. The Papagos ranged north to the banks of the Gila, and south to the Magdalena and Altar rivers. Within their own territory, the Papagos found permanent surface water flowing only short distances at a few especially favored spots. At Sonoita, on the present U.S.-Mexican boundary, a stream rose to flow a short distance before sinking into the sandy channel of a Pleistocene river. At Quito-baquito, farther west on the international boundary, permanent lakes and large springs allowed irrigation of agricultural fields. Else-where in the Papaguería, as the land of the Papagos came to be called in Spanish times, these Indians found only springs with sufficient flow to provide domestic water, rock tanks that held water after rainstorms. They deepened natural depressions in ephemeral stream beds so as to collect enough water to drink while cultivating flood-watered fields during the hot summer.

2

Small wonder, then, that the Papago people were termed the *Tohono au'autam* by their riverine dwelling relatives on the Gila, Santa Cruz, Altar and Magdalena rivers who spoke the same language. *Tohono Au'autam* may be translated as either "Thirsty People" or "Country People." To riverine speakers of the Northern Piman language, desert-dwelling Papagos indeed appeared to be a thirsty people. At the same time, because a riverine environment allowed greater affluence and urbanization, river-bank dwelling Northern Pimans tended to look down their noses at their poorer Papago relations. Hence the connotation that Papagos were rather rustic and countrified.

Religion helped Papago adjustment to desert life. Papagos regarded the July *náwai't* which "brought down the clouds" as the most important of all rituals. Each family collected ripe saguaro (giant cactus) fruit to boil into syrup. The Desert People enjoyed this harvest not only for its food, but also because girls' puberty ceremonies often brought a 4-day to month-long period of gaiety. Returning from cactus camps to summer fields villages, they contributed a share of their syrup to be fermented when village elders set a festival date. Elders brought sacred objects — eagle feathers, deer tails, beads and other fetishes — to place in the Council House with jars of fermenting syrup. To aid fermentation, villagers danced for two nights

3

outside the Council House to the music of rattles and rain-bringing songs sung four times. Dancers rested during the day. Summoned by messengers when the holy liquor was ready, the men sat in a circle to listen to "mocking bird" admonition speeches and to drink liquor served ceremonially by liquor-basket bearers. They served the cactus-jack saying, "Drink, my friend, to become beautifully intoxicated to bring wind and clouds here!" Imbibers responded to the mocking bird speeches with rain-bringing songs between each trip of the liquor-basket bearers. They drank until the cactus-jack ran out, including that which families dispensed from private stores during open houses.

To Papagos, the riverine Northern Piman Indians were the *Akimuhli Au'autam,* which may be translated as the "River People," or the "Flowing Water People." To the desert natives, the salient feature of riverine life was availability of life-giving fluid.

Undoubtedly the somewhat superior attitude of riverine Northern Pimans toward their desert-dwelling cousins stemmed from the economic dependence of Papagos upon the river valleys. The Papago people have for untold centuries depended upon the resources of the river valleys surrounding their desert to survive. Papago population long ago reached a density greater than their desert range could support at the standard of living the people desired. As a

4

consequence, the Desert People exchanged their labor and desert products they gathered and processed with their labor, for surplus foods produced in the river valleys by more sedentery Indians.

Despite the aridity of the Papaguería and the thorniness of its plant cover, the Thirst Enduring People managed to find there a variety of things to trade to River People for agricultural products to sustain them.

Most important were cactus fruits. The giant cactus yielded tiny glossy black seeds to trade. The Desert People boiled the juicy pulp down into a thick, sugary syrup like blackstrap molasses and stored it in round ceramic vessels for later barter as well as ceremonial fermentation. On occasion, they processed prickly pear cactus fruit into syrup in the same manner for use and export. Papagos traded to the River People cholla or "jumping" cactus mature fruits and buds picked when tender and dried. In southern Papaguería where the organ pipe cactus and "Old Man" cactus abounded, Papagos picked ripe fruits to trade or sell in Magdalena-Altar river settlements, as well as make into syrup. Giant cactus fruit loomed so important to Papagos that they reckoned their year from its harvest season.

A few favored slopes supported stands of Agave or "Century plant." When these started to bloom, the Desert People cut them from their roots, pit-roasted them, and dried the sweetish pulp for export. Leaves of the Agave and similar but much more widespread yucca yielded, when bruised, strong fibers for weaving rope and finer cords for making burden baskets. Papagos traded both the finished baskets and semi-processed materials for making them. They also profitted from labor intensification of stout desert plant leaves by manufacturing yucca leaf baskets and sleeping mats to change for foodstuffs.

A significant portion of Papago trade catered to the River People's taste for wild foods, including acorns, wild gourd seeds, peppers and wild potatoes.

Like many other impoverished populations, the Thirsty People traded animal protein for cheaper carbohydrates. Papago hunters and their families dried venison and mountain sheep mutton to trade to River People for cultivated products. They also tanned buckskins for export. A similar measure of Papago poverty was exportation of human hair cords. Some Papago families specialized in deer hunting. Professional hunters donned deerhead disguises, cooperated in the hunt, and sang hunting-magic songs to attract deer. They even dreamed of deer the night before a hunt. The Desert People themselves ate more rabbit than venison. They joined large community rabbit drives beginning with a ceremonial drive during the rain-bringing ceremony.

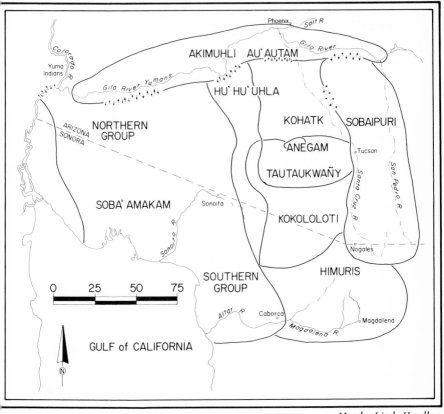

Map by Linda Handley

MAP 1 Northern Piman Indian Territorial-Dialect Groups at the time of initial Spanish contact late in the Seventeenth Century.

Papagos as descendents of the truly aboriginal occupants of the land. They are stereotyped as "Orphans," perhaps from the poverty of their territory, which did not give them easy access to any riverine area.

East of the "Orphans" in the desert south of the middle Gila River area intensively farmed by the Gila River Pima Indians, lay the lands of the *Kohatk* group. Genetically, this population lies between the River People and the Desert People because its members married people from both adjoining groups.

Immediately south of the *Kohatk* lies the large village of *Anegam*, whose origin legend records a migration from the river to this desert location.

South of Anegam one finds *Gu Achi*, largest of the purely Papago flood plain settlements, and the ceremonial center for what may be regarded as the historic core-area of the Papaguería. Gu Achi and its related settlements constitute the *Tautaukwañi* territorial group. This group's G-strings were always falling down, according to the general stereotype. These Papagos maintain the most distinctive religious shrine in all Papaguería. The oral scriptural account says a hunter tried to dig a badger out of a hole here. The hole enlarged and either a strong wind or flood of water emerged — various versions differ. After discussing the danger for four nights, people put their most valuable possessions in the hole to stop it up. Beads, eagle down and deer tails failed. People feared the earth would be destroyed. Then a wise man identified their truly most valuable possession. Four beautifully painted children placed in the hole ended its threat.

The people later erected a shrine to their lost children. A pile of flat rocks stands in an oval area perhaps 20 by 30 feet fenced by ocotillo wands. Every second year or so, the people renew the fence. No one knows how long ago they built the shrine, but the pile of discarded ocotillo outside the fence looms high on the flat desert.

Other settlements conducted growth ceremonies much like Christian rogation rites in intent. Only the Achi people and those at Quitobac in northern Sonora performed the elaborate *Wi'kita* ritual every fourth year. Its origin was attributed to *I'itoi,* the Papago "Elder Brother" or Creator, who planted prayer-sticks at both places. It had its own fetish, its own enclosure for secret preparation of ceremonial paraphernalia. Hereditary composers in each participating village "dreamed" new songs for each ritual. In the Achi region, five villages sang eight songs each. Ceremonial clowns provided comic relief from the tensions of the long rite. Achi celebrated *Wi'ikita* in winter, while

Quitobac held *Wi'ikita* in summer, closely resembling Puebloan dance-dramas aimed at weather-control.

South of the Tautaukwañi live the "Owl Cry People" or *Kokololoti*. They once occupied the desert southward in what is now northern Mexico to the banks of the Altar and Magdalena Rivers. In historic times, proximity to Mexican settlement in the river valleys exposed the Kokololoti to more Spanish-Mexican cultural influence than any other Papago territority entity.

In modern times, these populous territorial units have ranged eastward into mountainous territory between the Santa Cruz and San Pedro Rivers in southern Arizona. That area was earlier occupied by the Northern Piman speakers the Spaniards labeled *Sobaipuri*. The latter clearly followed a less completely sedentery way of life than the River People along the middle Gila or the Altar and Magdalena Rivers. They also made considerable use of upland resources. Historic epidemics decimated the Sobaipuris, while they bore the onslaught of the Apaches. The Papagos are generally a large people physically, and individual Sobaipuri leaders bested Apaches in individual combat when they first collided at the end of the 17th Century. Spanish colonial officials moved the San Pedro River Sobaipuris to missions on the Santa Cruz in 1762, however,

AN EARLY 20TH CENTURY EUROPEAN-STYLE SUNDRIED BRICK (ADOBE) HOUSE and utdoor living area shaded by a ramada.

A TRADITIONAL 19TH CENTURY GRASS-THATCHED PAPAGO HOUSE and household utensils showing that people lived mostly outdoors.

and the survivors intermarried with Desert People the missionaries recruited to repopulate their missions. Thus, it is not clear whether the modern eastward range of the Desert People reflects prehistoric territorial usage, or historic modification.

Life on the desert was not eternally grim. The Desert People worked and prayed and traded, but they also played. Intervillage races generated large-scale gambling, so more goods may have changed hands by wagering than by barter. Teams of two or three racers kicked an aboriginal style ball over a 10 to 15 mile course in one racing style much like that of the Pueblo Indians. Men ran in relays in another.

Races began with a challenge from one intervillage network to another. Both groups staged elaborate dramatic "skipping" dances to songs dreamed by village composers. The visitors ceremonially celebrated the names of important hosts to bring them good luck. Those they so honored responded with gifts, but their wives chased the visitors, pouring cactus syrup on their heads and tossing food at them.

When racing began next day, a shaman from each side watched over the pile of wagered goods. Men bet with men, women with women, often staking everything they had with them. The day-long race exhausted people's emotions, so winners quietly gathered their gains and left.

Spanish explorers first encountered Papagos in 1540, only 21 years after Cortez and his followers landed on the continent. The Spanish colonial frontier did not permanently reach Papago territory, however, for over two centuries. Then a Jesuit missionary established an outpost among the Himuris branch of the River People in 1687 and began exploratory journeys into the Papaguería. During the long decades between those two dates, the Thirst Enduring People did not continue living as their prehistoric ancestors had. Spanish colonial rule affected Papagos long before Spanish authorities finally arrived among them.

Prehistorically, a well-established trail along the west coast facilitated rapid diffusion of civilized concepts from the Middle American cultural heartland to the north. Via this route, Northern Piman speaking Indians received many of their principles of social organization, numerous economic techniques, implements and particularly sophisticated metal ornaments, and most importantly fundamental religious beliefs and ceremonial usages. When the Spaniards conquered the centers of native American civilization between 1519 and 1540, they left the relatively rural Northern Piman Indians hanging on the vine, so to speak, after its roots had been cut.

In the aftermath of military conquest, epidemic and initial colonial rule, powerful Indian groups on the northern marches of Middle America rebelled against the Spaniards in 1540. The Spaniards put down these rebellions in a costly "Mixton War" that thoroughly disrupted prehistoric trade routes between Middle America and more northerly peoples. Thereafter, the movement of both diseases and new ideas toward Papago country slowed. Not until the frontier of Spanish colonial rule approached the Papaguería did significant European influence penetrate to these Indians. Yet they probably abandoned during the interregnum a number of the more sophisticated religious practices most recently initiated under the influence of Middle American civilization.

As the Spanish mission frontier approached Northern Piman territory, these Indians reached out for contact. Missionary accounts recorded that parties of Northern Pimans ventured south to missions established among the neighboring Opatas to seek Catholic baptism. Magical cures with Holy Water were not the only thing Northern Pimas reached for. When missionaries finally reached Papago country, they found these Indians already growing wheat and watermelons, both Old World crops. So attractive were they to the Thirst Enduring People that these Indians obtained seeds from other Indians and began growing them even before Spaniards

18

reached their territory. The appeal of water-melons to the Thirsty People may be easily understood!

Papagos quickly planted wheat because it is a winter crop. The prehistoric Indian-cultivated plants — maize, beans, squash — are all summer crops that are not frost resistant. Wheat meant more food.

During long centuries of prehistoric Middle American influence upon Northern Piman Indians, the latter seem to have developed a marked inferiority complex. Throughout historic times, Northern Piman leaders have shown a rather surprising dependence upon external authority to sanction their leadership. Cut off from the well-springs of native American civilization after the Mixton War and other Spanish military actions, Northern Pimans reached out for colonial political support as well as new crops and miracle cures. Somehow, on their expeditions south to frontier Catholic missions, the Northern Pimans learned the importance to Spaniards of the symbol of the cross and ceremonial arches constructed for religious processions. By the time missionaries finally reached the Northern Piman deserts and rivers, both the Desert People and the River People knew how to welcome priests and military commanders with both symbols. Village leaders readily accepted the staffs symbolic of colonial authority handed out by Spanish authorities.

Father Kino's Christians. The pioneer Christian priest who established the first mission among Northern Pimans in 1687 was the Rev. Eusebio F. Kino, a Tyrolese Jesuit trained in Germany. Building a first mission among the Himuris whom Franciscans briefly visited half a century earlier, Kino soon explored widely along the streams that provided the River People with irrigation water and over the dry desert trails of the Thirst Enduring People. Kino quickly obtained additional Jesuit missionaries for the Northern Piman missions at San Ignacio and Caborca in the river valleys at the southern margin of Papaguería, setting the fundamental pattern of Spanish settlement that would be little modified during the next century and a half.

Apart from his geographic explorations which brought him contemporary frame, Kino worked at converting the Northern Piman Indians with many techniques familiar to much later missionaries. Kino coupled his Christian message about the afterlife with quite material contributions to bettering the standard of living of the Indians in this world. Kino carried wheat and watermelon seeds where they had not already penetrated. More importantly, he drove herds of horses and cattle from his missions and those of other Jesuits out to Northern Piman settlements to establish new grazing flocks and herds. Kino reported to his superiors that these efforts constituted economic foundations for future new missions for the conversion of the heathen natives. Until new missionaries arrived, however, these domestic animals out beyond the frontier of Spanish rule provided the Indians with a new source of animal protein in their diet, and with experience in managing cattle, riding horses, etc.

As cattle spread into the Papaguería not long after wheat, the Desert People capitalized upon their observations of Spanish technology and began to plow at least some of their wheat fields. They learned to carve the simple wooden "Egyptian" style plow that Spaniards from Andalusia brought to the New World. Papagos also began carving wooden shovels on the Spanish model. Maize-bean-squash cultivation continued on the basis of hills rather than rows, but a spade blade clearly worked better than the prehistoric digging stick. The Country People also expanded their trade with river valley residents with cattle products. They began to trade tallow and cheese as well as live animals.

Often accompanied on his explorations by contingents of royal troops, Kino helped military commanders on the colonial frontier forge a solid military alliance with the Northern Piman Indians to stand off the Apache avalanche.

German Jesuit Expansion. The Aspostle to the Pimas, Eusebio F. Kino, died in 1711. His colleague, Agustín de Campos, buried his body in a new chapel at Magdalena. The crusty Campos perservered at San Ignacio Mission until removed in 1736. Meanwhile, he had obtained reinforcements in 1732 when several Jesuits from the German Province established new missions, primarily along the Santa Cruz River northward into what is now southern Arizona on the eastern edge of the Papaguería. Some years later, one German Jesuit established the first Christian mission actually within Papago territory. Henry Ruhen carried the cross to the Sonoita oasis in the summer of 1751.

As the colonial frontier advanced in North-western New Spain, as this viceroyalty was called, Spanish authorities found themselves handicapped by serious Indian warfare on one flank. The frontier by-passed on the Gulf of California coast an embittered amalgam of small, tough bands of aboriginees who came to be known as the Seri. By the middle of the century, royal officials concluded that they must pacify the Seri in order to secure the northwestern frontier. The crown mobilized large forces, including a large contingent of Northern Piman auxiliaries led by Luis Oacpicagigua, and conducted a moderately successful campaign against the Gulf Coast hostiles in 1749. Oacpicagigua was rewarded by the civil-military authorities with the title of Captain General of the Northern Pimans, a uniform and evidently considerable respect.

The Pima Nativistic Movement of 1751. Unfortunately for the future tranquility of the Sonoran frontier, the Jesuit clergy running the Piman missions did not share the same values as the Spanish civil authorities. The military writ did not run in the missions. Rev. Ignacio X. Keller, the Jesuit missionary at Suamca, clashed physically with the Indian leader. Humiliated and incensed by the missionary's disregard for his military services to the crown, and indeed, his long efforts to persuade his fellow Indians to abandon their scattered desert settlements to move into the Catholic missions, Oacpicagigua returned to his native village of Saric. There he originated a bitter nativistic movement that sought to return his people to a pre-Spanish way of life that appeared increasingly attractive as the Indians learned more and more about European civilization from Spanish ranchers who had invaded their territory after the 1737 Planchas de Plata silver strike, as well as Jesuit missionaries and the military forces with which they had fought the mutual Seri enemy.

Already recognized by Spanish military authorities as an outstanding leader, Oacpicagigua sought a military solution to the "Spanish problem" facing his people. He did not retreat into futile magic as many a nativistic movement leader has before and since, but employed the same strategy of surprise attack that enabled

23

Pueblo Indians to oust the Spaniards from New Mexico in 1680. Oacpicagigua organized his forces in or near all the colonial missions and ranches that had been established within the territory of both the River People and the Desert People during the fall of 1751.

Oacpicagigua's security was broken by a few native Quislings a few days before the time he set for military action against the Spaniards. Most of the Spaniards warned of impending revolt by Northern Pimans scoffed apparently at the warnings, but two or three of the Jesuit missionaries heeded their convert friends and fled their missions in time to escape death. Early on the morning of 20 November 1751, the Indian forces organized by Oacpicagigua struck colonial missions and ranches throughout Northern Piman territory. Surprise was usually complete, and many ranch families were immediately wiped out. Only a handful of missions whose priests had heeded native defectors' warnings put up effective armed resistance to attack. These had to be abandoned by their defenders within a few days.

Before the end of 1751, the Spanish frontier had receded back to the edge of ancestral Northern Piman territory. Only San Ignacio and Magdalena, where the aboriginal population was by that time virtually extinct and had been replaced by Mestizos, Spaniards and Christianized Indians of more southerly tribes, re-

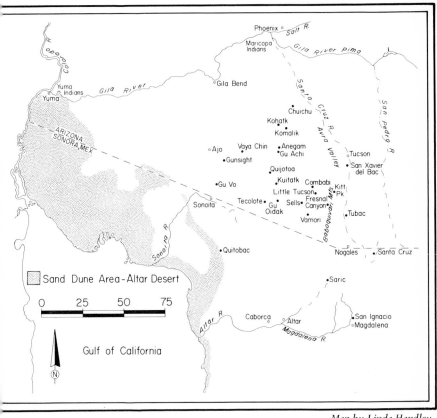

MAP 2 The Papaguería showing the extent of the true desert adjacent to the head of the Sea of Cortez, Papago settlements, Spanish missions and presidios and modern cities.

mained in Spanish hands. That mission and the civil settlement of Santa Anna a short distance to the south became the rallying area for the Governor of Sonora and his hastily augmented militia forces.

Frontier Fortification. Luis Oacpicagigua suffered the same handicap after his initial military success that had enabled the Spaniards to reconquer the New Mexico Pueblos in 1692. The Pueblo leaders proved unable to maintain their initial cooperation. Oacpicagigua's support evaporated. Significantly, once Oacpicagigua threw the Europeans out of Northern Piman territory, he lost the sanction of Spanish appointment that evidently greatly aided him in organizing the successful massacre of Spanish settlers. Although Spanish troops fought a few skirmishes with Oacpicagigua's forces, they had to win only one really pitched battle in order to open the way for resettlement of Northern Piman territory. Deciding that imperial authority over the rebel Indians could no longer rest solely upon the missions, the Governor of Sonora established two royal garrisons in 1752. Like the missionaries who usually followed river valleys, Governor Diego Ortiz Parrilla placed one garrison on the Altar River and the other on the Santa Cruz River at Tubac. Thus, Tubac became the first permanent Spanish settlement within modern Arizona.

By 1754, the Spaniards again effectively

26

dominated the southern and eastern riverine habitats of the Northern Piman Indians. They made no effort, however, to resettle in the territory of the Desert People. Military escorts reinstalled Jesuit missionaries in their riverine posts, but the Sonoita mission destroyed by Papago rebels remained in ruins.

During the decade following the nativistic movement of 1751, the Sobaipuris on the San Pedro River found themselves under increasing Apache attack. Their population had fallen throughout the first half of the century and continued to decline. Finally, Spanish military authorities had them abandon the San Pedro River Valley in 1762, resettling them in the missions along the Santa Cruz River where missionaries and colonial civil authorities had already been recruiting Papago migrants to replace the perishing native population. This Sobaipuri removal transformed the settlements along the Santa Cruz into the Apache frontier of Upper Pimería, and brought the Desert People quite directly into the defense of their entire territory, in alliance with Spanish troops stationed at Tubac.

Despite the presence of a Spanish garrison on this defensive line, the frontier was quite permeable, with Apache raids penetrating far into the Papaguería, and retaliatory expeditions by the Desert and River People striking high into the mountains to attack Apache rancherias.

27

Jesuit missionary accounts of Papago-Sobaipuri behavior during the middle 1760's make clear that the Indians continued to follow traditional economic patterns. Those who lived at San Xavier del Bac on the Santa Cruz stayed there during planting and irrigation season to raise their crops. They decamped to the giant cactus forests when fruit ripened at Papago New Year in July and struck out for the oak forests when acorns ripened and roved thick Agave stands when these plants began to push up their sugar-rich blossom stalks.

Franciscan Proselytizing. In 1767, Spanish King Charles III expelled the Jesuits from his overseas dominions. A year later, Franciscans from a convent in Querétaro arrived in Upper Pimería to carry on the program of converting Northern Piman Indians to Christianity. Like their Jesuit predecessors, the Franciscans never advanced the mission frontier beyond the river valleys into the Papaguería proper. The missionary at San Xavier del Bac did, however, reexplore the valleys and Papaguería seeking a land route to the Colorado River and California. Thus, Rev. Francisco T. H. Garcés M. laid the foundations for establishing missions among the Yuma where he was martyred in 1781, for overland expeditions to California, and founding a *presidio* at Tucson in 1776.

Although most of them received poverty-stricken missions, the Franciscans built up the cattle herds, encouraged Indian neophytes to cultivate mission fields, and recruited more Papagos to replace dying natives of the riverine missions. Within a decade after the Franciscans took charge of the Northern Pimería missions, they could consider launching church and convent construction programs. After 1780, the Franciscans replaced virtually every Jesuit church structure in Northern Pimería with a larger and more sumptuous Franciscan edifice. This large-scale construction program in the riverine settlements in the Santa Cruz and Magdalena and Altar River Valleys provided much employment for the Desert People who followed the age-old pattern of moving to the valleys at the agricultural harvest season or in periods of drought in the desert. The Thirst Enduring people during this period of relative plenty — the first enjoyed on this colonial frontier since the Spaniards reached it — probably received some wages in cash in addition to the traditional payment in kind that their Indian relatives had always made for their labor and desert products. In any event, the first term the Desert People applied to coins was *liahli*, which is a Northern Piman transliteration of the Spanish *real*, or "bit." The Northern Piman tongue simply could not twist itself around the Spanish initial trilled "R" and the unvoiced final consonant approximated the Spanish "L" fairly closely.

The pay rates for artisans on the frontier suggests that unskilled construction workers such as the Desert People would have been in that epoch would have been paid in *reales* rather than larger coins.

The Thirst Enduring People borrowed the Spanish word *peso* only considerably later in time when inflation had materially diluted the value of Mexican monetary units, making this larger coin sufficiently familiar to the Papagos for them to refer to it by its specific label rather than as *liahli*, which has the general meaning of "money." Papagos also transformed "peso" into "*pizh*".

Militarization. King Charles III initiated thorough-going reforms in the Spanish military establishment as well as the mission system. It took time for these to bring results, but a sharp shift in colonial policy toward hostile Indians on the northern frontier of New Spain occurred in 1786. Previously regarded as inevitable enemies, the Apaches had always before been fought when encountered. After 1786, the Spaniards negotiated peace agreements with Apache bands willing to settle beside military posts and subsist upon government rations and hunting instead of raiding. At the same time, the greatly strengthened frontier garrisons launched a series of multi-column invasions of Apachería that harried the enemy Indians in their formerly inviolate homeland, destroying houses and growing crops wherever found, killing adult male Apaches and capturing women and children whenever possible. The Spanish military command formed a Northern Piman company to garrison the old Tubac post, whose garrison had moved to Tucson in 1776, and participate in these search-and-destroy missions into the Apachería. Thus, many Northern Piman Indians, undoubtedly including some of the Desert People, learned Spanish battle tactics at first hand from Spanish officers seconded to the Indian company. They learned Spanish cavalry skills, and fashioned their lances and hide shields on Spanish models.

The Desert People nonetheless retained many non-Christian beliefs about warfare and enemies. When initiating military expeditions, Papago warriors deliberated in settlement council first. The Keeper of the Smoke admonished them to do their duty. The village crier usually accompanied the expedition. At an assembly point, he called the men to sit in a circle, with owl shamans who communicated with the dead in a smaller inner circle about a fire. Fighters who knew set ritual speeches delivered them. After war songs ended, the owl shamans predicted where enemies would be found.

Returning war parties entered a settlement at dawn, sending a messenger with trophies to announce who had slain or been slain. Girls streamed out to dance with weapons they seized from warriors, who had to redeem them with gifts. At the Council House, warriors boasted of exploits before going through 16 days of purification by earlier Enemy Slayers who sang over them. After purification, everyone joined in a victory dance which had its own "scalp songs" which referred to Buzzard. Pantomime dances around a war-trophy pole lasted the night through.

Band after band of Apaches surrendered under Spanish military pressure, and settled beside the posts at Tucson, Tubac, Santa Cruz, Bacoachi, Janos and El Paso during the late 1780's and early 1790's. By 1795, a Spanish column marched from Tucson to Zuñi Pueblo, only the second time direct overland communication occurred between the Sonoran and New Mexico Provinces since before the 1680 Pueblo Revolt.

As a result of successful Spanish pacification of the Western and Southern Apaches, the Papagos entered the 19th Century in an era of peace and prosperity. Old World diseases continued to depopulate the River People, and perhaps the Desert People as well. Yet the latter repeatedly responded to the call of Franciscan missionaries to move into the riverine missions to replace those who died.

MEXICAN PEASANTS

Life began to change for the Papago Indians again when Mexico won its political independence from Spain in 1821. The general installed as Emperor held onto his throne only until 1824, and then Mexico plunged into a long series of internal struggles over political power. So many military and financial resources disappeared in these political wars that the subsidies that purchased rations for the so-called "Tame Apaches" living at the frontier *presidios* tapered off and finally ceased. Quite understandably, as rations diminished and then stopped, the "Tame Apaches" gradually turned to hunting to eke out government fare, and then drifted away from the military posts and took up their former pattern of economic raiding. Having lived in the shadow of Spanish posts for thirty years, the observant Apaches had learned a very great deal about European arms, cavalry tactics and psychology, besides learning how to gamble at cards and acquiring a taste for distilled alcoholic beverages. Consequently, the Apaches who returned to the warpath in the late 1820's and early 1830's were considerably more effective guerilla raiders than their fathers and grandfathers. The "new Apaches" contemptuously referred to Mexicans as their "shepherds," raided them almost at will, and year after year forced the frontier of settlement southward.

The "new Apaches" did not, however, force the frontier of Northern Piman settlement westward. The Mexican garrison at Tucson anchored the defensive line along the Santa Cruz River, linked to southern sources of remount herds and munitions by the Mission San Xavier del Bac, now Papago in population, and the Tubac post. The Tucson garrison was backed up by the Papagos in the Pueblo of Tucson located near the foot of Signal Peak. The Gila River Pimas held the defensive line along the Gila River, and the Tautaukwañi group defended the desert frontier between Tucson and the Gila. The River People and Desert People alike turned more warlike, and restructured their society to meet the Apache war machine and hold their ancestral territory with Mexican assistance.

Legally, the Desert People became citizens of the Mexican Republic when the ideals of the French Revolution were translated into Mexican law. In practice, the beautiful French theories about the rights of man, and political equality for every citizen enabled literate Mexican Mestizos to despoil non-literate Mexicans of much of their land. Almost all Indians were illiterate at that time, although the Bishop of Sonora had begun to encourage clerical schools for Indians as early as 1803. Consequently, much of the land that changed hands had remained in Indian ownership under royal protection throughout the colonial period.

PAPAGO CHIEF CON QUIEN (standing in doorway) commanding squad of professional Papago warriors dressed in Spanish-Mexican military style. This historic photograph probably was taken late in the 1860's, and the figure in the foreground is not a Papago. Con Quien was principal war leader of the *Tautaukwañi* Papagos.

Chicanery over land tenure affected Northern Piman Indians only in the riverine irrigated farming areas, and a few desert mountain range mineralized areas. In both situations, the Desert People gladly labored for citizen entrepreneurs in the ageless peasant pattern. Nor did land losses seem to alienate the Desert People from the Mexican forces that fought Apaches as their allies.

During the 1830's the Tucson post encouraged Papago and Gila River Pima campaigns against Apaches. Teodoro Ramírez, an influential storekeeper in the small civilian population at Tucson, on occasion took Indian affairs into his own hands when the post commandant was strapped for funds or slow in encouraging the Indian allies. Northern Piman warriors who took to Tucson ears of slain Apaches as proof of their military success received recompense in the form of cartridges for their antique muskets, knives, cloth, cane alcohol and even Mexican dresses for their wives.

The Franciscan mission center at Magdalena emerged as another major magnet for the Desert People during the early Mexican period, if it had not already won that position. As independent Mexico expelled Spanish-born priests, the number of Franciscans in the Northern Pimería missions dropped finally to three priests, who concentrated at Magdalena, and traveled out from there on visits to the other churches. By

Photograph Henry F. Dobyns

"THE TWELVE APOSTLES" FESTIVAL committee at Mission St. Francis Xavier at Bac leads the procession from the church to the Indian dance pavilion and feast house on December second. Rotating committees lead Papago observance of the day of St. Francis Xavier each year, in the church that is now a national historical monument, and in their own stone feast-house.

this time, the cult of the statue of St. Francis in the Magdalena church was well established, and Papagos like other Sonorans went on a pilgrimage to the shrine when they could afford to do so.

As the missionary effort diminished, leaving the Desert People to their own religious devices for the most part, the Indians became strikingly self-reliant Catholics. When missionaries became scarce, if not before, devout Christian families in scattered desert rancherias began to build sun-dried brick chapels where they and other Catholic Papagos might worship in their own settlements.

Older women who made the tiring pilgrimage to Magdalena for the festival of St. Francis on October 4 carefully memorized the Spanish words and music for the rosary, so they could sing and chant for their own people at home. At San Xavier del Bac, ritual responsibility devolved upon a revolving Committee of Twelve Apostles charged with conducting the festival of St. Francis Xavier on 2 December and several other ceremonies. Each male committeeman actually brought to the ritual cycle not only his own labor and financial resources, but also those of his wife for cooking and serving the delicious feasts the people enjoyed on these occasions.

Altar and Caborca, where the old curmudgeon Spanish priest Faustino Gonzales remained for many years despite the edicts of nationalist authorities in far-off Mexico City, also drew Desert People during the years of Mexican sovereignty. The increasingly Mexican and Mexicanized farmers along the Altar River continued to hire Papago harvest hands just as their riverine Indian predecessors had for ages past. For the Sand People, Caborca provided a market for the Indian child-slaves they traded from their Yuma captors. Some Mestizo residents of Caborca entered into this traffic in human flesh, and some Yumas traveled to Caborca for direct sales. Probably the Sand People profited significantly from this northwestern frontier trade.

The difficulties over succession to political office that plagued the Mexican Republic also increasingly agitated its northwesternmost State of Sonora as the initial grip of the frontier garrison officer cadre loosened with the passage of time. Armed political campaigning reached such a pass that the Desert People were treated as rebels in 1843 after one gubernatorial fight. A punitive expedition marched north along the western margin of the Baboquivari Mountains into the very heart of Papaguería. Some of the Desert People took refuge at Magdalena; others confided in their symbiotic relationship with the Tucson garrison.

An unsettled state of affairs continued for another decade, during which Mexico lost a war with the United States while Sonora was absorbed with its Indian campaigns. The 1848 peace treaty fixed Mexico's new northern boundary along the Gila River, making the Papaguería the district immediately south of the new international boundary. In 1853, enemy forces from the U. S. side of the boundary achieved their deepest penetration into Papaguería, and their bloodiest success in attacking a settlement of Desert People.

The invading force approached the mountain spring settlement of Mesquite Root while most of its male inhabitants were absent. Although one or more children spied the assailants, they failed to identify them as hostile. When warning was finally given, an old man herded some women and children into the council house and defended its door until he was killed. The attackers then fired the structure and burned alive those who had taken refuge within. They massacred the Desert People scattered in the other houses, taking captive a few exceptionally attractive young women.

One of these captives later escaped from the enemy column as it retreated, found her way back to other Papagos, and related her account of the disaster. Another young girl who hid under a bush eluded the attackers, and also ran off to find other Papagos and relate her skimpy account.

That same year, the U. S. negotiated the Gadsden Purchase of the tract south of the Gila River to the present international boundary.

40

This split the Papaguería with about two-thirds in the U. S. and one-third in Mexico.

UNITED STATES DOMINATION

As the United States slowly moved troops into the Gadsden Purchase Area, it found Northern Piman Indians to be eager allies against marauding Apaches. The first 20 years of U. S. sovereignty in the Purchase Area saw federal troops finally defeat the Western Apache bands with the aid of allied Papago, Gila River Pima and Maricopa warriors. Beginning late in the 1850's, the federal government also began to supply the friendly Indians with agricultural implements and arms. Friendly Papagos guided Anglo-American travelers who strayed into the nearly waterless Papaguería from water-source to water-source during this period. By 1872, the Apaches were formally pacified, although U. S. troops pursued small Chiricahua bands until 1886 and the last post created to fight Apaches was not deactiviated until after World War I.

San Xavier Reservation. Concentrating upon pacification of the Apaches, federal policy makers quickly assigned those hostile Indians to reservations where they were confined by U. S. cavalry detachments. Those same policy makers moved much more slowly to guarantee to friendly Papagos any land base at all not treated as part of the public domain open to Anglo-American settlement. Finally in 1874, the federal government created a small reservation (71,065 acres) around Mission San Xavier del Bac. That was rather too conspicuous a landmark to overlook, with a bellicose population of Papagos that had steadfastly helped to defend the Santa Cruz Valley line against the Apaches. An Indian Agent appointed at this reservation began additional issues of agricultural implements such as plows, hay rakes, hay cutters and eventually wagons.

Soon after Tucson came under the U. S. flag, U. S. citizens began to move there and to open a variety of businesses that attracted increasing Papago custom. Freight lines channeled retail goods from California and Sonora into Tucson in the 1850's, greatly augmenting the supply of consumer goods available there. Papagos found that they could exchange their coarse but durable water vessels for Anglo-American products. Water stored in these clay pots slowly seeped through to evaporate on the exterior, thus cooling the remaining contents, a highly desirable characteristic on the hot semi-desert prior to mechanical refrigeration. Papago potters traveled all over southern Arizona after Apache pacification as Anglo-American settlement spread over the Gadsden Purchase Area, making their vessels and selling them all over southern Arizona Territory. The ceramic trade continued to be profitable to Papago potters well into the

TWO PAPAGO WOMEN selling ceramic vessels on the sidewalk of a southern Arizona town in 1900. They carry bean boiling pots and water cooling *ollas* in their *kihau* or backpack frames, and wear Spanish-Mexican peasant style clothing.

present century when electric refrigerators came into wide use.

For a short time, Papago salt expeditions to the Gulf of California supplied nearly all of the salt moving in southern Arizona trade. The religious journeys to the Gulf became commercial ventures as well, and men took pack-horses along to haul larger quantities of salt. In other words, Papagos quickly entered into the cash economy of the Anglo-Americans who assumed control of the Gadsden Purchase Area, using U. S. coins and currency, as well as Mexican.

At the same time, the Kokololoti continued to trade with the Mexicans in Sonora. They gathered *pitahaya* (Organ Pipe cactus) fruit when it ripened and sold it at public markets in Mexican settlements. They packed salt to those markets, and pots as well. The Desert People continued to make the pilgrimage to St. Francis in Magdalena, maintaining their awareness of Roman Catholicism, other Indian believers such as Yaqui and Mayo vow-paying dancers, the Spanish language, Mexican manufactured goods, alcoholic beverages and coinage.

Papagos also continued to work in the harvests of the Gila River Pimas, who enjoyed a twenty-year agricultural boom growing produce and grain for sale to the overland travelers taking the Gila River route from eastern states to California, and to early settlers in southern

Arizona. The Gila River Valley afforded Papagos even more work, paid for in cash, when the transcontinental Southern Pacific Railroad was built across the edge of their territory. Some Huhu'uhla labored on construction crews, learning how to work horses in harness, how to drive wagons, manipulate fresnos, and so on. With this paid on-the-job training in managing a new transport technology, some Papagos began to purchase wagons which stimulated a whole series of changes in sex roles among the Desert People. Men took over such former women's tasks as water-hauling with barrels on wagons, and firewood cutting.

Once the railroad was completed, Tucson gained rapidly in population and the price of manufactured goods fell as transportation costs diminished. The Tucson market was integrated into the U. S. national market, to the cost of the long-time Sonoran suppliers. Thus, Papagos began to purchase U. S. manufactured goods, including such complex items as sewing machines, although they long continued to wear the Mexican peasant-style clothing they had donned during an earlier period.

During the first railroad decade, a number of Anglo-American ranchers moved herds into the Papagueria. Still grateful to the Whites for their pacification of the Apaches, the Desert People apparently did not overtly oppose this graziers' invasion of their homeland.

During the same decade of the 1880's, several mining camps sprang up within Papago territory to exploit fairly rich lode ore deposits. Quijotoa mine camp became a booming place for a few brief years, as did Gunsight and Comobabi and other prospects. The processing required water, as did the miners, who therefore dug deep wells to tap subterranean waters. Thus, Anglo-Americans introduced another new technological resource-tap to the Thirst Enduring People. After the ore lodes played out and the miners abandoned their camps, the Thirst Enduring People moved near the deep wells and somewhat reduced their thirst endurance.

During this same decade, a Presbyterian missionary began to proselytize among Gila River Pimas, winning some influence among the Desert People. A few Papago families began to send children to Presbyterian boarding school at Tucson, and even to the federal government school at Carlisle Barracks, Pennsylvania. Thus a few Papagos became literate in English for the first time.

Papago Resurgence. By the middle 1890's, the attitude of the Desert People toward Anglo-Americans and Mexicans began to change markedly. Numerous factors contributed to Papago aggressiveness in maintaining and recovering land tenure rights, water rights, and utilizing deep well waters. The economic depression that struck the United States in 1893

PAPAGO WOODCUTTERS with a wagon load of firewood from desert hardwood trees to sell in town for cash.

seriously depressed the market for Arizona range cattle, so that many cattlemen simply went broke. Some abandoned their herds in Papago territory, so the Indians easily founded their own herds from abandoned stock. Owning livestock motivated Papagos to spread out over their land so as to take advantage of sparse pasturage. At the same time, twenty years of peace brought a marked increase in population, so that there were more Papago mouths to feed in the 1890's than there had been in the 1870's or the 1850's. The Desert People spread out again as population pressure mounted. The pacification of the Apaches removed a physical and psychological threat that had long inhibited scattered settlement. On the other hand, the rural police force organized in Mexico under President Porfirio Díaz began to exert considerable pressure on the Mexican Papagos during that decade. Relations between Mexicans and Papagos deteriorated so seriously that one group of Desert People actually organized an armed raid on a small Sonoran town. After that open breach, many Sonoran Papagos fled north across the international boundary into southern Arizona to escape the wrath of the dread Mexican *Rurales.*

Papago armed action probably possessed many of the elements of a nativistic movement to get back to the "good old days" that had been present in the 1751 assault on colonial Spaniards and the slaying of Jesuit missionary

F. X. Saeta at Caborca in 1695. On the other hand, the dominance of Anglo-Americans had become so clear by the 1890's that for the first time Papagos participated in the purely magical behaviors of a millenarian end-of-the-world cult. Enough young Desert People had attended Presbyterian boarding schools of religious-oriented federal schools to constitute a significant body susceptible to the influence of a millenarian prophet. In this case, the prophet seems to have been black. In any event, almost all the Papagos in one Kokololoti settlement sold or abandoned their homes and goods, and moved to the top of a hill farther north to await Judgement Day. One family that traditionally provided leadership in the village sold off nearly all its livestock for money with which to purchase food to maintain 40 to 50 believers. After waiting for weeks on end, the people gradually realized that Judgement was not quite on the prophet's schedule, and the movement collapsed.

Still, Presbyterians proselytized effectively, winning a following organized in native congregations primarily in the Kokololoti area. This denomination encouraged Papagos to translate hymns into their own language, trained native missionaries who led congregations in the little reservation churches. Formally educated young men also banded together in what they called the "Good Government League" to work toward persuading the federal government to reserve lands for the Papagos and aid schools, hospitals and water development.

At San Xavier, the Bureau of Indian Affairs alloted reservation lands to individuals in accord with the General Allotment Act of 1887. Although this action created tremendous legal confusion over ownership of fields as lands were inherited later on, immediate impact of allotment was minimal. Papagos did not sell their allotments.

Federal Land Guarantee. The U. S. government began to set aside portions of the Papaguería as Papago Indian Reservation in 1911. Major increments to the reserved area came in 1912 and 1916, but the process of guaranteeing Papago occupancy of a large contiguous area continued for some years after that. The main Papago Reservation contains 2,774,370 acres, about the size of Connecticut. Even when completed in 1940, this process failed to provide federal protection for anything approaching the original territory of the Desert People in the United States. The federal government itself assumed proprietorship of the Organ Pipe National Monument, apparently deeming protection of an exotic cactus more important than confirming aboriginal Papago land rights. The cacti protected grow abundantly across the international boundary in northwestern Mexico and are in no danger of extinction. Moreover,

50

zealous U. S. National Park Service officials evicted Papago families living at the permanent water at Quitobaquito partly within the monument and partly within Mexico regardless of their aboriginal occupancy rights.

The territory of the Sand People, including the rich Ajo ore deposits, remained in private ownership or U. S. public domain, much of it used as an air force gunnery range during and since World War II. The corridor of irrigable lands in the Casa Grande Valley between the Kohatk and the Gila River stayed in White ownership, as did the Avra Valley and all of the rich Santa Cruz River Valley outside the old San Xavier Reservation. Thus, even though it eventually did act very tardily to guarantee its Papago allies in the Apache wars part of their aboriginal territory, the federal government reserved for them far less and far poorer land than it awarded the hostile Apaches, allowing the majority of the mineral wealth and irrigable lands to be exploited by non-Indians. Congress did not convey mineral rights in even the reserved areas to the Papagos until 1955.

The federal government carried out one program of technical assistance for the Thirst Enduring People during the score of years from 1912 to 1933, that they much appreciated and which fundamentally altered their life way. The government purchased or drilled a total of 32 deep wells to obtain permanent domestic water supplies for Papago settlements in the alluvial valleys where flood farming produced food crops. These wells allowed the Thirst Enduring People to live permanently in the field villages if they wished to do so, leaving the mountain spring settlements to grazier families that needed to graze their livestock on the grass and browse at the higher elevations. Living close to permanent and abundant water supplies, the Thirst Enduring People also could relax their stringent cultural norms for conserving water, and drink all that they wished.

Deep tube wells and powerful pumps installed by the government also permitted irrigation agriculture on a small scale at San Xavier and Chuichu near the northern edge of Kohatk territory. The wells and pumps at San Xavier represented a federal attempt to revive native cultivation in the Santa Cruz River Valley destroyed by Anglo-Americans. Copious springs once provided abundant irrigation water channeled to the fields in surface ditches. Not long before the turn of the century, Anglo-American farmers dug galleries downstream from Bac to augment flow into their irrigation ditches. The subsurface galleries allowed the annual floods to cut into the valley alluvium, so the river rapidly scoured a deep, wide and usually dry channel. The water table dropped to the level of the bottom of the new channel, so springs dried up, leaving Papago fields quite literally high and dry.

Western Ways Photograph by Charles W. Herbert

MAIZE AND SQUASH HARVEST from San Xavier District field irrigated by water from government wells. As soon as Jesuit missionary Eusebio F. Kino saw Bac in 1692, he recognized it as one of the most fertile riverine areas in Pimeria Alta. When irrigated, its fields continue to yield abundantly.

Even wells the Indians used to obtain potable domestic water went dry. Thus, the Bac irrigation wells constituted a federal effort to restore Papago agriculture that White greed and ecological ignorance had destroyed. These wells have never been markedly successful, however, partly because the people have always regarded wells and pumps installed at government expense as government property. Papagos also resent paying irrigation water fees for "White" water to replace natural water White men stupidly destroyed. Wage labor in Tucson offers a more attractive alternative.

As automobiles became increasingly important in the U. S., the federal government, the state of Arizona and Pima and Pinal counties began to construct roads across the growing Papago Indian Reservation. While the automobile was transforming White society, the horse-drawn wagon reached its apogee among the Desert People. Inasmuch as many urban homes in southern Arizona were heated with wood-burning stoves, many Papagos earned most of their cash income cutting mesquite wood and hauling it to town in wagons for sale.

In the fall, long caravans of wagons covered with white canvas stretched over their bows, collected on the wagon trails leading south through the reservation gates in the international boundary to Magdalena. Where once lone men hiked or rode horseback on the pilgrimage to the

54

shrine of St. Francis, whole families journeyed together on wagons to the Mexican town. In their wagons, the Desert People reverently carried their inexpensive religious prints and statues of Catholic saints to press against the recumbent statue of St. Francis as they filed past its catafalque. They believed that this physical contact transferred some of the miraculous curative power of St. Francis to these religious prints and statues and ribbons they kept on their household shrines. When finances permitted them to do so, Papago pilgrims purchased new statues of saints from religious art work factories in Mexico City or fresh lithoprints from Checkoslovakian presses. Indian families also enjoyed the secular fair that accompanied the festival — the ferris wheel, merry-go-round and other rides, the colorful woven goods, beautiful hand-crafted saddles and boots, spicy festive foods, and especially delicious Mexican beer, mescal and tequila that Indians could not legally consume in the United States until 1953.

As the federal government gradually reserved portions of aboriginal Papago territory for the Desert People's continued use, it also worked toward social and cultural integration via formal education. Government day schools appeared in many newly stabilized field villages where numerous children lived, supplementing pioneer Catholic schools founded by Rev. Bonaventure Oblasser, O. F. M. Federal officials and missionaries continued to recruit children to attend various boarding schools, but during this period of expanding Bureau of Indian Affairs services, most Papago children attending school studied in classrooms in their home villages.

While the federal government reserved more and more land to Papago use, it enlarged its Bureau of Indian Affairs bureaucracy charged with carrying out federal trusteeship for that land, operating the day schools, and drilling the deep tube wells. Local representatives of the Bureau oftentimes behaved as though only the Great White Father in Washington and his local minions knew what was best for the Desert People. They had manifestly not learned the lesson of the Santa Cruz River Valley subterranean irrigation galleries with their disastrous environmental consequence. They did not recognize that technologies and social structures suited to Anglo-Americans and a well-watered environment would not necessarily work in the Sonoran Desert among native Indians who had learned to survive in that relatively hostile environment through untold centuries of close observation of nature and cultural adjustment to it.

The policies and actions of federal bureaucrats assigned to the growing Papago Indian Reservation often appeared arbitrary, authoritarian and mistaken. A number of older village headmen formed the "League of Papago Chiefs"

Photograph by Henry F. Dobyns

LOOKING FROM THE PORTAL of a new arcade around the central square of Magdalena de Kino, Sonora, Mexico, toward the parish church and monument over the grave of pioneer missionary Eusebio F. Kino, S. J. Papago pilgrims visit the recumbent statue of St. Francis Xavier in the church. Devout pilgrims often test their state of grace by trying to lift the statue, believing that they are unable to do so if their previous year's sins are unforgiven. The statue is made from light materials, yet some pilgrims cannot lift it.

to oppose the Good Government League and its pro-government tendencies. By the mid 1920's the Chiefs wielded sufficient power to oust a Bureau of Indian Affairs superintendent whom they opposed.

Clashing on numerous policy issues, the two grass-roots organizations generated a good deal of ill feeling toward each other that lingered long after the organizations themselves dissolved. Nonetheless, the pressure that both groups brought to bear upon the Bureau of Indian Affairs appears to have had a salutory effect in moderating an authoritarian decision-making process.

New Deal Reformation. When President Franklin D. Roosevelt began in 1933 his reordering of national priorities and procedures labeled the "New Deal," he appointed John Collier Commissioner of Indian Affairs. Collier reformed federal Indian policy, serving until the end of World War II. He achieved a remarkable change of direction on many reservations including the Papago jurisdiction.

When the Roosevelt administration established the Civilian Conservation Corps to employ young jobless men under military discipline on environmental improvement projects, Collier managed to have an Indian Division included. He anticipated that without a special Indian Division, the CCC would inevitably exclude most if not all eligible Indians. The CCC-Indian Division strikingly affected the Desert People.

Under Collier's leadership and the influence of an energetic reservation superintendent, the CCC operating on the Papago Indian Reservation identified and developed work projects in consultation with local Indians. This consultation process significantly strengthened the councils elected to govern each of the eleven districts into which the reservations had been divided. These had originally been fenced off as cattle grazing districts. Naturally enough in the Sonoran Desert environment, the concern of the Papagos continued to be water, so probably the most important achievements of the Papago CCC program lay in water resource development.

During a decade of CCC action, more new wells were drilled than the 32 that the Bureau of Indian Affairs had provided during the previous 20 years. Inasmuch as the domestic water requirements of the Desert People had already been mostly met by the Bureau's program, however, most CCC wells provided water for livestock. They were equipped with windmills to pump water into storage tanks supplying stock watering troughs.

Not all portions of the Papaguería possess subterranean waters at depths allowing economic pumping and many areas simply lack subterranean water. On the other hand, cattle cannot gain weight if they must walk many miles to water. Thus, wells and windmills could not open up to grazing all of the stands of native pasturage on the reservations. The CCC-Indian Division turned, therefore, to excavating *charcos*. *"Charco"* is a Spanish term for a waterhole, and in Papaguería denotes an artifically-deepened pond catching ephemeral stream flow following a rainstorm. The Desert People had excavated small *charcos* with hand tools to augment the domestic water supply at the valley fields for unknown centuries. When they obtained fresnos and trained their ponies to pull these excavation implements in the 1880's, they enlarged many charcos. The CCC charco excavation program of the 1930's again went beyond domestic water needs to sink numerous charcos in small cachment basins where surface runoff stored in a waterhole would enable cattle to graze surrounding forage.

The CCC-Indian Division excavated charcos with mechanized equipment so these and similar projects enabled young Papago men to learn how to operate heavy equipment and to qualify for jobs not previously open to them.

The CCC contributed significantly to improving communications on the Papago Indian Reservation by improving existing roads and trails, building new ones, and installing additional telephone lines. Thus, the CCC constituted a major influence toward technological change among Papagos.

Important sociological shifts occurred during the same period of national economic depression. Low wages on the farms in the irrigated valleys around the Papaguería, and the lack of employment for Indians there, forced the Desert People to depend heavily upon subsistence flood farming. The Bureau of Indian Affairs expanded its technical assistance programs for agriculture under Collier's leadership. The Papago Agency added an Agricultural Extension Division and a Soil and Moisture Conservation Division during the 1930's. Technicians in these new activities initiated numerous programs aiming toward improving and increasing production on reservation lands.

Recognizing that overstocking had seriously overgrazed the scanty pasturage and browse on parts of the Papago Indian Reservation, the new technicians encouraged the Desert People to reduce their livestock numbers while improving animal quality. Because many horses ran wild or nearly so, the Bureau of Indian Affairs carried out a horse reduction program designed to remove from the range as many unbroken and unused horses as possible. The Bureau also conducted a cattle repayment program to improve the quality of Papago animals. In other words, the Bureau exchanged high quality cows for tough, rangy Spanish type cattle people turned in.

In agriculture, Anglo-American technicians observed closed-basin flood irrigation agriculture in Mexico. There seasonal overflow from major streams allowed commercial crop production from a single flooding of fields, termed *bolsas,* enclosed by a high enbankment. Technicians promoted the *bolsa* system on the Papago Indian Reservation in cooperation with the CCC-Indian Division. Half a dozen closed flood irrigation basins were constructed. Papago farmers successfully raised subsistence crops in some of them. Others proved to be technical failures, the largest of them finally being destroyed by a flood. Papagos constructed no such basin on their own, even though hundreds of flood farmers raised subsistence crops with the age-old techniques of *akchin* agriculture during the depression. *Akchin* irrigation utilizes the natural flow on the deltas of ephemeral streams, with minimal Papago diking and ditching to control flooding.

Commissioner Collier's Indian New Deal included keystone legislation passed by Congress to reorient the relationship between the federal government and Indians living on reservations. The Indian Reorganization Act of 1934 encouraged Indians to establish reservation government where these did not exist. Responding to that Congressional initiative, the Desert People in 1936 drew up a constitution and by-laws then approved by popular vote. These documents provided for a Tribal Chairman, and a governing Council made up of two delegates elected from each district. Geographically separate San Xavier constitued a district, as did Gila Bend.

As the Papago Tribal Council began to operate in January of 1937, it provided a level of political organization standing between the ordinary Indian citizen and the federal bureaucracy. Councilmen elected José Ignacio chairman. He served four 1-year terms. Many delegates had been politically active in the League of Papago Chiefs or the Good Government League. Consequently, much of the Council leadership was already experienced in representing the interests of the Papago people.

The CCC-Indian Division of the Papago Indian Reservation having systematically consulted people assembled in district meetings in planning its projects, the district councils wielded more power than the fledgling Tribal Council prior to the second World War. The relative strength of the local councils stemmed directly from their patronage. The CCC-Indian Division was the largest single employer on the reservations, and possessed the greatest pool of economic development funds, more even than the Papago Indian

Agency. Thus, key decisions about employment, projects, and all sorts of benefits came at the district rather than the total reservation level.

At the same time, the CCC constituted a considerable force working toward future social and cultural unification of the Desert People. Young men recruited from all parts of the reservations lived together in CCC camps. They learned that age-old stereotypes either did not apply to individuals or were quite irrelevant. Living and talking together intimately, the young men tended to develop a common Papago dialect, dropping traditional colloquialisms in each of the long-standing territorial-dialect divisions. The whole CCC experience generated, moreover, a euphoric feeling among the young men. They ate abundantly and regularly while many of their relatives and Anglo-Americans elsewhere struggled to keep from starving. They earned cash wages while cash was extremely scarce, and because Papago poverty had long been acute, their CCC wages often exceeded the cash income any one in their families ever earned before. This relative affluence made young men more independent of their older relatives than they otherwise could have been. Their acquisition of skills previously unknown to any of the Desert People reinforced that independence. Thus, the psychologically rewarding CCC work experience conditioned most of those Papagos who participated in it toward

64

seeking reservation-wide solutions to what they could perceive as reservation-wide problems, using forms of social organization and technology novel to Papago historic experience up until that time.

World War II. The second World War fundamentally changed the relationship of the Papagos to the rest of the world. First of all, a relatively large number of young Papago men served in the U. S. armed forces, traveling all over the world. This wartime experience greatly broadened their intellectual horizons, and generated in them a feeling of belonging to the nation as a whole. Secondly, wartime demand for cotton drew those Papagos who remained at home fully into the national cash labor market and relative prosperity.

During the depression, mostly Anglo-American families forced to abandon the Midwestern Dust Bowl turned to migrant farm labor to survive. Numbers of them provided the hand labor to harvest expending fields of irrigated short staple cotton in southern Arizona, moving on to the Pacific Coast fruit harvests. After the U. S. entered the war, armed forces mobilization withdrew millions of able-bodied men from the labor pool. Then rapid expansion of the aircraft industry in the Middle West and southern California created industrial jobs for the remaining migrant laborers. By the fall of 1942, the cotton growers of southern Arizona, who had greatly expanded plantings to supply wartime fiber demands, found themselves without harvest hands. They desperately turned to Japanese-Americans interned at Poston in the Parker Valley on the Colorado River and Gila River Relocation Center, and to the reservation Indians of southern Arizona. Cotton growers and labor contractors churned up clouds of dust on Papago Indian Reservation roads as they recruited cotton pickers to salvage the vitally needed and economically valuable crop. The Desert People comprised one of the largest reservoirs of underemployed labor in the Southwest in 1941, but by the end of 1942 the Papago labor force was largely commited to agricultural production on irrigated fields in the Gila and Santa Cruz River Valleys. The Desert People returned, in other words, to the age-old economic pattern they and their ancestors followed from time immemorial. They simply mobilized a larger agricultural work force than ever before, earning higher cash payments for unskilled work than ever before.

Despite grower pressures on pickers to harvest the huge cotton crops as rapidly as possible, the Desert people coped their own way. They picked cotton at a steady pace. An occasional Anglo-American or Black picker blessed with great manual dexterity might race through a field and place 400 to 500 pounds of fiber on the paymaster's scales by the end of the day.

Adult Papago pickers consistently weighed in 200 to 300 pounds of fiber per day — day after day after day, without risking heat exhaustion under the blazing fall sun.

The devout Catholic Desert People made plain to growers, moreover, that the Magdalena pilgrimage took precedence over even national patriotism and personal gain. Faced with Papago intransigence, most growers quickly decided to haul their Indian pilgrims to Magdalena in trucks rather than let them spend time making the trek in slow horse-drawn wagons. Thus began a shift from wagon trails to highways, from wagons to trucks, pickups and buses for pilgrimage. Papago pilgrims continued to enjoy the secular fair as long as their funds held out, feasting, drinking, purchasing consumer goods, watching enthralled Yaqui and Mayo Indian deer and *pascola* (clown) dancers from southern Sonora pay their vows.

Peter Blaine led the Tribal Council in 1941-42 as Bureau of Indian Affairs male employees went to war. Demand for meat fostered price increases paid to Papago stockmen until federal price controls went into effect. Higher prices encouraged stockmen to sell off culls, thus reducing some of the grazing pressure on reservation lands. As the cattle market improved, the Tribal Council in 1943 under Chairman Henry A. Throssell, instituted a sales inspection and certification service to protect both buyer and seller. A 3% tax on livestock sales financed it and produced some of the first significant income for tribal government. José Ignacio returned as Chairman in 1945-46.

Post-War Era. The Desert People moved into the post-war years with much of the optimism that characterized the U. S. citizenry as a whole. The high morale of the immediate post-war years dissipated to a considerable extent as goals and expectations formulated in wartime were frustrated during the following 20 years.

In 1947, a high official of the Bureau of Indian Affairs announced a policy change aimed toward removing the federal bureaucracy from Indian land trusteeship. Responding to Congressional dissatisfaction with never-ending appropriations for the Bureau, that organization proposed to "terminate" federal services to Indians. It suggested a list of reservation populations culturally prepared for immediate termination, another list of those that might be terminated in five to 10 years, and a third to be terminated in from 10 to 25 years. Despite strenuous efforts by the Bureau under former Commissioner Collier, the largest Indian group in the country, the Navajos, clearly fell into the latter category. Disastrous winter storms in Navajo country in 1948-1949 caused a number of deaths and emergency conditions widely publicized by newspapers opposing federal foreign aid proposals. Two years of drought then turned the crises even more acute. Public concern sufficed to move Congress to authorize and later to fund a Navajo Rehabilitation Program.

Placed also in the third termination category, the Papagos realized that in fact they would need a large-scale rehabilitation effort much like that instituted for the Navajos if they were to be able to achieve a reasonable standard of living and pay for substitutes for federal services. The Papaguería was also in the grip of a severe drought, and stock owners hauled feed and water to their weakening animals. Fortunately, a young Papago shipyard worker with some college training in engineering returned to the reservation on vacation and pitched into the drought relief effort. Recognizing the great leadership potential of Thomas A. Segundo, the Papagos in 1947 elected him Chairman of the Tribal Council. That body in 1948 made its chairmanship a full-time job paid $2,400 per year. Re-elected, Segundo quit the Bureau of Indians Affairs where he had found a job to sustain himself and his family to labor full time for the tribe. Under Segundo's leadership, numerous hard-working planning committees developed a long-range Papago rehabilitation plan completed in 1949.

Unfortunately for the Desert People, their plight never received national publicity. Moreover, the environmental crisis of the Papaguería was both perennial and creeping. The region is too warm to suffer from disastrous snow storms that make newspaper headlines. Even the best headline writer cannot make much of the crucial fact that evaporation from unshaded water in the Papaguería averages nine feet per year. Some Democratic Congressmen introduced bills for Papago rehabilitation, and some high Democratic officials visited the Papago Indian Reservation to promise support for them. Nevertheless, the quiet and permanent environmental crisis of the Papaguería and its native inhabitants escaped newspaper notice. Consequently, not enough public clamour ever occurred to persuade Congress to pass the Papago bills.

The environmental crisis of the Papaguería never alters. It only deepens as the Papago people are integrated into U. S. society through public schooling, listening to advertisments of the affluent society on transistorized radios, and viewing it in Anglo-American dominated cities and towns surrounding the Papago Indian Reservation. Since the end of the second World War, Papagos have progressively emigrated from the desert to well-watered and affluent river valley and mine towns. By the beginning of the 1970's, no more than half the Papago people resided on the three reserved areas. They fall into five economic groups.

Economically best-off are the wage workers, relatively better educated than the rest of the Papago people, fluently bilingual or sometimes

70

even monolingual in English, having been reared in households striving to forget the Papago heritage. Most Papago wage workers live and work in Sells, the administrative town where Bureau of Indian Affairs offices, Papago Tribal offices, and Public Health Service facilities are all concentrated. Traders and cattle buyers headquartered in Sells employ other Papagos. Kitt Peak National Observatory opened late in November of 1962 east of Sells at the margin of the reservation, employing over 20 Papagos. Few more than a dozen Papagos work for traders and schools at Santa Rosa and other reservation settlements, indicating the massive concentration of wage workers at Sells.

The second largest group of wage workers lives on San Xavier Reservation just south of Tucson. Papagos residing there work in a wide range of enterprises in the urban Tucson area, and for the U. S. Public Health Service, OEO pre-school program and Mission itself on the reservation.

As the federal Great Society programs geared up during the latter half of the 1960's, the Papago reservation payroll outside San Xavier District was estimated at $1,000,000 annually with some 200 permanent and 70 part-time workers.

At that time, perhaps 250 Papago cattlemen constituted a second major economic group. Only about 30 of them earned an adequate living, however, from full-time cattle husbandry. These few families constituted a prosperous and politically powerful group. The far more numerous small owners ranching part-time necessarily supplemented their income with temporary wage work off the reservation, temporary reservation jobs or subsistence farming. They comprised the third economic group on the reservation. In 1966, gross cattle income brought Papagos approximately $650,000 annually, disproportionately distributed.

Some 300 to 500 Papago families without cattle earned their cash by seasonal and temporary wage work outside the reservation, even though they regarded themselves as reservation residents. Many still engaged in subsistence agriculture on flood-watered fields. Papago women made enough baskets to sell about 3,000 per year at the beginning of the 1970's. The tribal Arts and Crafts Board had been struggling since at least 1963 to dissuade basketmakers from employing such non-Papago substances as hair dye and shoe polish to blacken martynia design elements. Annual income per capita averaged only $700 on the reservation at that time. Little of that income came from craft sales. One couple in San Xavier District, for example, lived from art and craft work. Domingo Franco relied mainly on lamp bases fashioned from cholla cactus wood. He painted primitive scenes and he and his wife Chepa

Photograph Courtesy Arizona Historical Society

ʌPAGO WOMAN SEWING together the base of a coiled basket of yucca leaves and
artynia (Devil's Claw) seed-pod skin. Finished baskets beside her are of same
ɑaterials. She cuts green leaves from wild yucca plants and bleaches them white in
ɪe sun. She cultivates or purchases from another Papago black skin from the seed
ɔds of domesticated *Martynia* plants, which grow longer than the wild variety.

dressed cholla-wood Papago dolls to make a living.

Papagos receiving unearned income comprised the fifth reservation economic group. Most receive welfare assistance and are not in the labor force. By 1962, 266 Papagos were receiving old age assistance, 154 aid to dependent children, 12 aid to the blind and 104 general assistance. Thus, the welfare group bulked larger in numbers than any other economic group on the reservation. This figure reinforces the fundamental importance of the riverine areas to Papago life.

That half of the Papago population which has migrated from the desert to work and live in mine towns and agricultural villages in southern Arizona thus carries, along with other taxpayers, a relatively heavy burden of welfare costs. Remittances in the form of welfare payments and family funds sent to relatives undoubtedly permit Papagos to remain in desert villages today who under earlier economic conditions would have had to move to riverine areas to seek employment. Yet the age-old pattern of environmental imbalance between desert and river valley has been but little modified by such remittances.

Disheartened by federal failure to enact a Papago rehabilitation program, and feeling that he might be more successful if he just knew more, Tribal Chairman Segundo resigned in

1953 to move to Chicago to enroll for further study at the University of Chicago. Studying law and social science, Segundo became caught up in the rapidly emerging urban Indian movement in the Windy City. He served as director of the All-Indian Center there before going to work for the state of Illinois. Enos J. Francisco became chairman from June, 1953 through 1954.

Before his departure, Segundo had started the Papago Tribe working on legal action against the United States for unfair and unconscionable dealing in incorporating most of the Papaguería into the public domain, and belatedly reserving only a portion of it for its native inhabitants. Congress passed an Indian Claims Commission Act in 1946 enabling any Indian group with such a grievance to file suit before a special Indian Claims Commission. Segundo's administration retained attorneys to prosecute the Papago claim, and the author initiated ethnohistorical research on the Papago behalf in the spring of 1952. Dr. Bernard L. Fontana and other researchers carried on under Claims Counsel Royal D. Marks of Phoenix, and his Washington associates. The case was finally heard by the Commission in 1964. Yet only in 1970 did the member of the Commission responsible for the Papago case announce a recommended $27,000,000 award to the Desert People for the loss of 6,000,000 acres at 1916 land values.

Lobbying for the rehabilitation bills, and dealing with other political crises of the late 1940's and the 1950's persuaded Segundo and other Papago leaders that they needed non-Indian support. In response to the Papago quest, a group of concerned urban residents of Tucson formed an Association for Papago Affairs to assist the Papagos. With a core of intellectuals at the University of Arizona, this organization has had a strong interest in research, yet accomplished significant public education in the area.

Another kind of limitation on Bureau of Indian Affairs monopoly on federal services to Papagos occurred when President Dwight Eisenhower transferred responsibility for Indian health from the Bureau to the U. S. Public Health Service in 1955. One consequence of that change was eventual reconstruction of a hospital in Sells. The Indian Bureau hospital built there in 1921 burned down in 1947. Not until 1960 did USPHS erect a new hospital at Sells to serve thousands of Papago patients with more than mobile clinics and the far-distant hospital at San Xavier Mission, or Santa Rosa 1959 clinic.

From 1955 to 1965, the Papago people endured a decade of further technological change in the dominant society, with a concomitant deterioration in Papago economy. During this period, large mining corporations negotiated agreements with the Papago Tribe to dig huge open pits on the San Xavier Reservation and to sink new deep shafts near the northern end of the main reserved area. These agreements brought the tribal government added and sorely needed stabilizing income. In 1963, however, agricultural as well as mining leases still brought the tribe only $5,000 of its $85,400 estimated annual income. Some San Xavier District families benefitted from royalty payments for individually held lands stemming from the 1891 individual allotments made under provisions of the Dawes Act. Most Papagos, on the other hand, received little or no direct benefit from the mines.

A series of dedicated Papagos provided tribal leadership. Patient, steady, Mark Manuel led from January, 1955. Regaining the chairmanship in 1959, Enos J. Francisco served until 1963. He defended Papago giant cactus fruit harvesting in Saguaro National Monument. The federal government granted $400,000 in 1962 for erosion control, road construction and building forest fire breaks, heralding things to come.

Then Sells District Councilman Eugene J. Johnson, an employee of Kitt Peak National Observatory, won the February 1963 election. He gained re-election a year later with Oliver K. Moristo as Vice-Chairman. Johnson fostered range clearing, fencing and water storage. He struggled to retain federal aid for Papagos moving to off-reservation towns to work. During his administration, the tribe borrowed $10,000 to construct a new Sells post office, repaying the loan from federal rentals. It also built community centers at Santa Rosa and Pisinemo, partly with Bureau of Indian Affairs contract funds.

Baptist minister Robert C. Mackett won the chairmanship in February of 1965. He won re-election the next year and again in 1967. That year Mackett led a movement to oust the Bureau of Indian Affairs local superintendent, a Sioux Indian. The Bureau proved less responsive than it was in the 1920's.

The Tribal Council set an example for other jurisdictions in the spring of 1966 when it elected a woman as judge of the Tribal Court. The Council chose Mabel Antone over eight male candidates. Then 41, Mrs. Antone had worked as a teacher's aide in the Sells pre-school program. Her father, José X. Pablo, was long a prominent leader and one of the framers of the tribal constitution. Re-elected to two-year terms in 1968 and 1970, Judge Mabel Antone became widely respected for her judicial decisions. Most cases she hears involve alcoholic beverage possession or drunkenness and disorderliness. She has spoken out in favor of ending Papago reservation prohibition in order to ease alcohol-related problems. Bootlegging had become a serious problem on the Papago reservations by at least 1965. Bootleggers then sold an estimated 40 to 50 cases of wine each week, even to children as young as 10 years of age.

Two years before the Council named Mabel Antone to the bench, women in San Xavier District had achieved another sort of distinction. Early in 1964, they received their charter as the first federated woman's club in the United States composed entirely of native Americans.

The Great Society. The Lyndon B. Johnson national administration brought to the Papago people the same wide range of new federal programs that dramatically altered life on Indian reservations throughout the country. This change stemmed from legislation Congress enacted at the President's urging to strive toward a "Great Society."

To many Papago leaders, enabling legislation for the U. S. Office of Economic Opportunity appeared to have been written especially for Papago Indians. The law called for people themselves to meet and to plan what they wanted to do with federal funds to improve their own lot. The legislation looked on the surface as though it called for precisely what Papagos had done for centuries, what they did with the Civilian Conservation Corps — Indian Division during the 1930's, what they had done with the Production Marketing Administration during the 1940's to improve the range, and what they hoped to do in formulating their rehabilitation plans published in 1949.

Reading the act, reservation leaders thought of the man who led the great planning effort that culminated in the 1949 Navajo-style rehabilitation plan that Congress never adopted. If anyone could seize on the opportunity implied in the act, they reasoned, Thomas A. Segundo was that person. So they asked Tommy to return to the Papago Reservation to help draft the initial Papago proposals to the Office of Economic opportunity. He agreed. He returned, and once again plunged into the maelstrom of Papago planning, looking farsightedly into a future to be achieved through Papago efforts reinforced by massive federal funding.

The proposals Segundo helped prepare won prompt approval from OEO. The promise Papagos thought they had perceived in the enabling act really existed! Once federal funding was assured, many Papagos wanted Thomas A. Segundo back to lead the efforts the OEO agreed to finance. After returning to Chicago feeling that he had finished the proposal-writing task, Tom Segundo once again answered the call of his people. He left the Illinois Highway Department job and urban life he and his family enjoyed to return to the desert. From English-speaking Illinois, he turned to the frenetic English-Spanish-Papago-Yaqui-speaking Tucson and reservation populations. An exploding OEO financed Papago force soon burst out of the tribal headquarters building erected a generation earlier into a covey of office trailers in Sells plus urban offices in Tucson.

As Director of the Community Action Program, Segundo formulated a set of community development principles based upon his experience as tribal chairman and study with social scientists at the Universities of Arizona and Chicago. "The OEO Act called for maximum feasible involvement of the people. This is tailor-made for the Papago people, because that is the way we do things. The Chairman in the Tribal Council cannot approve an action without reference to the people. The Chairman lends support, submits things to the Tribal Council, and full discussion follows. The Tribal Council seldom gives instant approval. Instead, a proposal must go to the district meeting. . .

"Anything done with the people must involve everybody. There must not be programs without involvement of the people. The jobs must not be doled out as political plums. . . .

"We must be willing to take one step back to take ten tomorrow. You cannot ramrod anything through — it takes time, but when a decision is reached it is a decision of the people. We will never break any speed records, but we are building solidly so our work will not come apart at the seams."

81

By the summer of 1966, the Papago community action program had achieved significant momentum, according to a University of Arizona evaluation, in spite of the involvement of the people in all deliberation.

The following year, Papago leaders told CAP Director Segundo much the same thing native Americans on other reservations told their OEO directors. The best tribal leadership was sorely needed in the tribal chairman's office, not the OEO office.

Heeding the call, Segundo in 1967 campaigned for the chairmanship of the Tribal Council. The man who had been the youngest tribal chairman in the country almost a generation earlier won easily. Early in February, Segundo once again took office as chairman. This 1968 election also notably brought women onto the Tribal Council representing San Xavier and supposedly conservative Hickiwan Districts. In his inaugural message, Segundo pledged "our best effort to help you help yourselves in your long struggle, year-in and year-out, against our common enemies: poverty, disease, ignorance and lack of opportunity for development. Our progress in the past has been slow, for there are cultural and traditional factors to be accommodated. So our present endeavors will take time. Perhaps this administration may not even see the fruit of our labors, but let us all join together in our common effort to lead our

Papago people, invoking the blessing and help of our God."

Later that year, Democratic gubernatorial candidate Sam Goddard resigned as an alternate delegate to his party's national convention with a plea that Segundo replace him so Arizona Indians would be represented. Thus state politicians noted the return to Arizona of an Indian leader who had been a delegate to a previous convention.

Toward the end of 1968, a member of the Tribal Council brought another aspect of U. S. government policy to public attention. An Army representative visited Sells to decorate Councilman Raymond A. Lopez of Santa Cruz village with the Army Commendation Medal for heroism under fire in South Vietnam. Segundo convoked a special council meeting for the occasion, the first such event resulting from the Vietnam conflict.

Thomas A. Segundo won annual re-election through 1971. Thus extending his administration, he maintained a nearly impossible daily schedule. In the spring of 1971, he answered a request from Papago students attending Dartmouth College to come speak to them. Rushed as usual, Segundo started to drive to Phoenix to board a transcontinental flight. He and tribal education director Josiah Moore thought all feeder airline flights had already left the Tucson airport. Moore drove to Phoenix and boarded an east coast flight. Segundo checked, discovered an Apache Airlines flight running late, and boarded it. On that tragic sixth day of May, the last Apache Airlines flight in history dived full-speed into the ground near Coolidge, Arizona, killing everyone on board. Thomas A. Segundo became the first Papago Tribal Chairman to die in office, giving his life in the devoted service of his Desert People. More than 6,000 Papagos sadly attended the funeral at Baboquivari High School in Sells, while Roman Catholic priests, Prostestant ministers, tribal officials and the author spoke in an ecumenical spirit that allowed every Papago to honor his departed leader in his own way.

Brief descriptions of some of the "Great Society" programs underway among the Desert People will indicate the kinds of change occurring.

Anglo-Saxon Protestants supposedly suffer from a Puritan Ethic demanding hard work, saving, thrift, and moral behavior. While most Papagos profess Roman Catholicism, they also live by values that foster hard work, thrift and morality. The Tribal Work Experience Program initiated in 1967 well illustrates their bent. Papagos who formerly received welfare checks committed themselves to work from 8 a.m. to 5 p.m. five days per week all year for an extra $30. By early 1970, Papago Tribal Work Experience Program employed 325 persons in 45 settlements, nearly half of those on the reservations. Participants worked as road builders, carpenters, water line layers, well repairers, bricklayers, equipment repairmen, cooks, mechanics, school, police and hospital aides. Some villages assigned road repair top priority, while others preferred health projects or home construction. A glance back at the figures on Papagos in each reservation economic class reveals how important this program alone was in cutting the size of the welfare class, and increasing the size of the wage-earning class.

After working for 10 years as property supply clerk among Pima Indians, Augustine Lopez returned to the Papago Reservation to head the TWEP. Elected Vice-Chairman of the Papago Tribal Council, he succeeded Segundo in May of 1971. Then he won election to a term in his own right in 1972. Successful administration of a "Great Society" program again qualified a candidate for tribal leadership.

Recognizing the key importance of English language education for young Papagos, the tribal government moved quickly to take advantage of federal willingness to finance preschool instruction. It persuaded the Office of Economic Opportunity to provide $128,834 for a nine-month Head Start program for the 1966-67 school year. Over 100 children in Sells, Santa Rosa, Chuichu, Pisinemo, Vaya Chin, Gu Vo and San Xavier benefited. Only a year before, the

University of Arizona's Bureau of Ethnic Research found that 975 Papago school-age children were not in school. Bureau Director William H. Kelly estimated that 400 to 500 lacked a "legitimate" reason, but cultural dissonance constituted a major motivation to avoid the classroom. Head Start sought to lessen that dissonance, and continues to do so.

Proceeding as Segundo put it, one pace back in order to progress 10 forward, Papagos began discussing housing needs under federal programs in 1965. Early in 1966, Chairman Mackett presented a study of reservation housing to the Tribal Council, which debated creating a housing authority. The Gila Bend District tribal councilmen initiated action in mid-1967 to create the authority. They had strong motivation — 42 families in their district wanted new homes.

Early in 1969, the Authority was surveying sites for 70 homes at Gila Bend, San Xavier and Sells. By the end of the year, Housing Authority Chairman Elee Sam had roughly one million U. S. Department of Housing and Urban Development dollars in the bank for 30 homes at Gila Bend, 25 at San Xavier, 25 at Sells and 12 at Chuichu.

At the end of 1970, HUD granted the Papago Housing Authority $1,438,800 to finance 30 homes for Sells, 15 for Santa Rosa, 10 for Chuichu, 10 for Pisinemo, 12 for Kohatk, 13 for Komalik and 10 more on the Gila Bend Reservation. At Sells, where need for new housing seemed greatest, some families erected wood and sun-dried brick homes under self-help programs. Finally in the spring of 1971, the Papago Indian Housing Authority, now led by Andrew Patricio, requested 50 low-income single-family modular homes with two to five bedrooms for the reservation capital. The Department of Housing and Urban Development awarded the Authority a $1,008,968 contract to set up prefabricated units. The Authority assumes responsibility for maintenance and management of these units, for rent collection and for occupant selection.

Looking toward modernization of village public as well as private buildings, Papago officials in September of 1967 obtained $164,000 from the U. S. Economic Development Administration to establish five new community centers. Two years later, the U. S. Office of Economic Opportunity was financing a community organization and neighborhood center program at a $170,000 level. With medical projects added to community development, OEO grants rose to over one quarter of a million dollars in 1970. One outstanding leader in the Papago community action program has been Mrs. Lupe José, who returned to Anegam village after working for several years in California. She has been much in demand as a delegate to regional and national conferences.

Office of Economic Opportunity grants also

enabled the Papago Tribe to establish Papago Legal Services to furnish free legal aid to reservation residents, alcoholism rehabilitation, and emergency food program.

Public Secondary School. The pace of Papago deliberation is well illustrated by the history of establishing a public high school on the Papago Reservation. The Bureau of Indian Affairs proposed the idea in 1962, and Chairman Enos J. Francisco heartily endorsed it. There was no high school on the reservation, so students had to attend boarding school in Phoenix, California or Colorado, or move to Arizona towns. New Chairman Eugene Johnson cautioned proponents to proceed slowly. The Indian Oasis School Board chairman in March 1963 urged filing application for federal funds before 30 June. The Pima County Supervisers added 494 square miles to the district, making it the county's largest with 882 square miles. The District began adding grades so that it offered instruction through tenth grade by 1967-68. Then, following six years of discussion, the District won a $780,000 grant from the U. S. Office of Education to begin construction of a high school. Then 1971 brought a $1.8 million grant, and opening.

THE FUTURE

The Papago people long ago chose to live in so ecologically extreme an environment that their entire known past provides sure clues to their future. The aridity of the desert Papagueria will continue to shape the future of the Desert People just as it has shaped their past. The villages scattered about the thorny desert will continue to grow more children than can making a living in them. Family fecundity among recent migrants to cities and towns will continue to be high. Thus, Papagos will continue to migrate from the desert settlements to the riverine areas of economic prosperity east and north of the Papagueria, and to the Ajo and San Xavier District mines. The eternal verities of low rainfall, lack of surface water, and a limited number of mountain springs have been somewhat altered by deep tube wells in the alluvial valleys. Still, water remains a sharply limiting factor in Papagueria. Today, it is reinforced by public education in the English language that opens many windows on affluent U. S. society outside the desert, with its numerous attractions.

What has changed most drastically in the environment of the Papagos is migration of Mexican-Americans, Anglo-Americans and Blacks into the same riverine valleys where the Papagos historically and prehistorically supplemented desert resources.

Non-Papago migrants into the Santa Cruz and Gila River Valleys have taken up the fertile and well-watered lands Papagos once could exploit seasonally. They are dependent on fast-falling subterranean water supplies tapped by deep tube wells, yet seemingly unable to stem the flow of new arrivals and limit population to the hydrologic carrying capacity of the margins of the Sonoran Desert. Thus, the future of the Papago people is gravely prejudiced by the non-Indians who find the edges of their immemorial territory climatically and scenically attractive as well as economically profitable.

While the environmental crises of the great Colorado Desert becomes steadily more acute, the Papago people face future needs for adjusting to U. S. society through formal education. National society will not tolerate non-literate peasants. It demands commercial, not subsistence, farming. It will make traditional flood-farming steadily less and less attractive to Papago peasants, motivating them to migrate off the desert and learn new skills in order to find employment in commercial agriculture or other sectors of the economy. National society will make traditional part-time cattle ranching and craft production, including basket-making, steadily less attractive in the Papaguería, displacing ranchers' sons into wage labor or white collar work. More and more formal education will become a prerequisite to making a successful shift from traditional economic activities to the ones that will sustain the Papago people in the future.

90

Courtesy of Arizona Historical Society

ROMAN CATHOLIC NUNS began instructing Papago children at San Xavier del Bac a century ago. Several missions on the Papago Indian Reservation operate small schools for local Papago children. Most Papago school children today attend reservation schools operated by the Bureau of Indian Affairs or the huge Public School District 40 in Pima County, or public schools in cities and towns such as Ajo, Tucson, Eloy, Coolidge and Casa Grande.

The future of the Papago people as part of the native American minority in U. S. society will not be easy. The Papago way has for many centuries been to proceed with deliberate, not all possible, speed. Such is the course of wisdom under a blazing desert sun that can fell a man in a hurry with heat prostration. The rush and bustle of urban society is directly antithetical to the Papago way.

The Papago way has in historic times involved relaxed extended family life almost out of sight and sound of other families in small desert hamlets. Families taught their children proper Papago manners by example and admonition, and the difference between Papago and Anglo-American manners creates and will continue to create problems for the Papago wage earner. The apartment living of the contemporary metropolis again seems antithetical to Papago values and habits. So does the superficial camaraderie of the world of commerce.

The Papago obtaining off-reservation employment will often be criticized for his dress. The Papago who can afford it strives to be neat, but often turns away from clerical "white shirt and tie" jobs. The Papago often seems quiet to other people. He typically concentrates on his job, and not on how often he can open his mouth. Thus, he will seem rude to those who miss a conventional and meaningless "Good Morning" or who are uncomfortable with the 30-second Papago response-interval (compared to less than five among Whites).

To the casual Anglo-American, the Papago who does not introduce himself to everyone will frequently appear uncivil. Yet Papagos are amused by handshaking outside religious ceremonies, and are trained to consider it highly impolite to look directly at a newcomer, much less to ask him his name! Brought up to reciprocate gifts and actions, Papagos possess no word of their own with the meaning of English "thank you." They will often be regarded as ungrateful, therefore, for lack of casual conversational coin, while the recipient of real reciprocity overlooks the deeper meaning of actions while focusing upon words, or their absence.

Increasing amounts of formal education of more and more diversified types will clearly be a major route by which young Papagos will leave their scattered villages to move into urban future society. Many Papago students will emulate Grace Cachora, who graduated from Maricopa Technical College as a dental technician in 1971 after three years of hard work. Her college level education required near-heroic determination, and a public fund-raising campaign plus Congressional pressure on a Bureau of Indian Affairs that failed to process her financial aid application. Other Papago students will require less assistance, but some will need the kind of public support that rallied to Miss Cachora.

Other Papago students will in time follow the trail into Western medicine being blazed by Clifford Pablo. He graduated from Phoenix Union High School's practical nursing program in 1967, because it was the only nursing school that he could find that would accept men. After working for two years in the Sells hospital, Pablo enrolled in the University of Arizona College of Nursing. Aided by a tribal scholarship, Pablo works three shifts per week at Pima County Hospital to help finance his college degree. Once he completes the four-year nursing degree program, he plans to seek a medical degree.

Quite likely a few Papago students will in the future follow Joaquín Lopez into the ministry. This first Papago ordained in the Presbyterian Church achieved this distinction in 1947 at Vamori Village. Probably a few will emulate a Papago nun in the Roman Catholic faith. Others may find secular employment through Mormon missionary efforts. Surely sectarian conflicts loom in the Papago future, for they have already begun.

No sooner was construction begun on Baboquivari High School than sectarian difficulties arose in the school district. In 1968, the Southwest Indian Mission of the Church of Jesus Christ of Latter-Day Saints recruited 18 Papago children to live with Mormon families and attend Los Angeles public schools. Each Indian child removed from reservation school cost the district money, inasmuch as the state paid some $800 annually for each enrolled pupil. The District that year hired Don L. Peterson as superintendent. An active member of the Church of Jesus Christ of Latter-Day Saints, Peterson replaced half the teachers with fellow Mormons within two school years. Before an audience of 300 parents and children, Peterson reportedly stated that he sought to convert all school children to his faith. The Mormon missionaries active among Papagos met at his home, and publicly stated their goal of recruiting 200 Papago children for the Mormon youth program. By the spring of 1970, parental displeasure with Peterson brought 400 Papagos to a protest meeting. The school board notified Peterson that his contract would not be renewed. During 1970, every member of the all-Papago District 40 School Board was challenged by a recall election, but only one incumbent failed to win. Thus, early in 1971 the Board organized with Antone Chico as its president, continued Claude Miguel as its clerk, with Tribal Judge Mabel Antone, education director Josiah Moore and Ricardo Manuel completing its roster. The Board continued Peterson in office. Papagos have learned the bitterness of local school board electioneering with sharply opposed factions, contrary to the Papago way. Future sectarian conflicts may confidently be anticipated!

AERIAL VIEW OF THE CAPITAL of the Papago Indian Reservation, Sells, named fo
former commissioner of Indian Affairs. Baboquivari Peak, sacred to the Des

ople, dominates the mountain range on the skyline which extends south (to the
ht) into the state of Sonora, Mexico.

The immediate future for the urbanizing Papago people acquiring much more formal education than any of their forebears contains dark clouds of other kinds. Too many are delayed or injured or killed in automobile accidents.

Even though automobiles pose greater dangers to the Papago people than the horses introduced to them by Spaniards or the wagons acquired from Anglo-Americans, they are absolute necessities in the Papago present and future. For transportation in the desert Papaguería will predictably remain a fundamental prerequisite for Papago participation in U. S. society. Learning more about automotive technology lies over the Papago horizon. The new Pima College in Tucson already began to act to aid Papago learning about automobiles early in 1971. It dispatched two teachers with a truck, tools and parts to the reservation on Saturdays. Visiting Little Tucson, Big Fields, Santa Rosa and Gu Vo, the instructors sought to make the Papagos more self-sufficient by teaching them how to keep their automobiles running. Many vehicles on the reservation did not run, yet could be put into operation with relatively minor repairs. As innovations occur in land transportation, Papagos will necessarily learn more and more about transportation technology, in order to maintain their mobility within the three million acre reservations and their neighborhoods.

The mines already opened on Papago reserva-

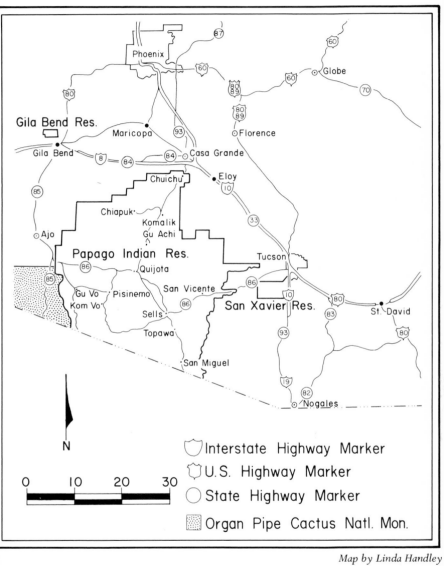

MAP 3 The Papago Indian Reservation, the Gila Bend Reservation, and the San Xavier Reservation in southern Arizona.

tion lands and now nearing production will provide a limited number of jobs for Papagos in the immediate future, expanding the vital wage worker sector of the labor force. This should prove beneficial. At the same time, the mining corporations pay royalties to the tribe, placing a firm economic base under tribal government and services, which certainly will be helpful in working toward an improved Papago future. Yet, the companies also pay royalties to individuals on the San Xavier Reservation who were alloted land or inherited it individually. Such unearned income will not necessarily improve the future of those receiving it. Just as many Osage families came to grief when tremendous oil royalties brought them large unearned incomes after 1907 (See THE OSAGE PEOPLE), so San Xavier Papago families appear in many cases to be headed for unhappy experiences as their mineral royalties pile up.

The future of the Papago people would really be bright were the technological genius of U. S. society able to discover an economic basis for continued life in the seventy-odd small, scattered Papago hamlets in the reserved areas. The Office of Economic Opportunity has already begun training other Southwestern Indians to utilize hydroponic farming technology to grow high economic return specialty crops. Can even hydroponics provide economic returns where water is so absolutely scarce as in Papaguería?

Mexico has already pioneered technology for

THE ENVIRONMENTAL CRISIS of the Papaguería is permanent, as these cattle skeletons on the Papago Indian Reservation indicate. These cattle fell victim to a "drought," but droughts occur frequently and animal husbandry is always a risky form of economic enterprise for Papagos.

tapping geothermal energy in the Sonoran Desert. Subterranean exploration might locate geothermal energy resources beneath the Papaguería to power industry or other developments to benefit Papagos.

Such developments are purely speculative at this time. What U. S. society could do to improve reasonable prospects for future Papago economic rewards in the desert would be to initiate a large-scale program of research in many disciplines on the economic utilization of plants and animals that have adapted to life in the desert environment as have the Desert People themsleves. Despite massive federal investments in agricultural research in Arizona, these have overwhelmingly investigated crops and techniques for irrigated farming. The United States has followed an engineer's path of building water-storage dams and reservoirs, and huge canal distribution systems, and genetically selecting plants for heavy irrigation production. It has not studied desert flood farming nor unirrigated plant cultivation. Unless modern science is to admit defeat by the desert environment, some alternatives must be found to the Western engineering approach of the past. Without alternatives that would allow the Desert People to remain in their desert and even return there from the cities, their future increasingly lies in becoming chocolate skinned, tall, heavyset White men. Is that the best future the U. S. can hold out to the Thirst Enduring People?

GREAT SEAL OF THE
PAPAGO TRIBE

The Papago tribal seal shows sacred Baboquivari Peak the legendary home of I'Itoi, the Papago Creator, at its center. In the foreground appear examples of thorny desert plants, especially the saguaro or giant cactus, which yielded the Desert People rich red fruit from which they made syrup and "cactus jack" to drink in rain-bringing ceremonies. Eleven stars surrounding this view represent eleven electoral districts into which the three Papago reservations are divided. With the words "Great Seal of the Papago Tribe" around the rim appears the date "1937." That was the year when the Papago Tribal Council began to function in January under a Constitution and By-Laws adopted the year before under provisions of the Indian Reorganization Act of 1934.

SUGGESTED READINGS

Unlike Navajos, Papagos have not been exhaustively studied by anthropologists and historians. Much information about Papagos is scattered, out of print or in archives. Several fundamental reports are out of print, but may be consulted in large libraries.

DOBYNS, HENRY F., *Papagos in the Cotton Fields, 1950.* Tucson: Author, 1951.

Description of seasonal harvest labor after World War II before picking machines displaced Papago hands.

FONTANA, BERNARD L. AND OTHERS, *Papago Indian Pottery.* Seattle, American Ethnological Society, 1962.

Technical analysis of one Papago craft.

JOSEPH, ALICE, ROSAMUND SPICER & JANE CHESKY, *The Desert People.* Chicago: University of Chicago Press, 1949.

Report of study of Indian personality conducted during World War II, based on residence in two villages, and extensive psychological testing of children.

LUMHOLTZ, CARL, *New Trails in Mexico.* New York: Chas. Scribner's, 1912. (1971 Río Grande Press reprint has new foreword by Dr. B. L. Fontana)

Extensive account by pioneer enthnographer who visited widely in Sonora to the Sea of Cortez, and in Arizona Papago settlements. Enchanting presentation.

SPICER, EDWARD H., *Cycles of Conquest: The Impact of Spain, Mexico, and the United States on the Indians of the Southwest 1533-1960.* Tucson: University of Arizona Press, 1962.

Best Southwest area summary of socio-political process yet published, with outstanding summary of Papago cultural history.

UNDERHILL, RUTH M., *A Papago Calendar Record.* University of New Mexico Bulletin, Anthropological Series, 1938.

English version of Papago rendering of mnomic marks on a "calendar stick," which Northern Pimans used to keep track of important past events.

Social Organization of the Papago Indians. New York: Columbia University Press, 1939.

Basic work on Papago socio-political structure by anthropologist who spent more time studying Papagos than any other.

Papago Indian Religion. New York: Columbia University Press, 1946.

Basic work on Papago religion as practiced historically, slighting Roman Catholic influences.

THE AUTHOR

 HENRY F. DOBYNS, Professor of Anthropology at Prescott College, studied Papago economic and political structure from 1947 to 1953, and has accumulated information about Papago history until this writing. From 1959 to 1966, he served with the Department of Anthropology of Cornell University in Peru, Ecuador, and Bolivia, as well as on its Ithaca campus. Chairman of the Department of Anthropology at the University of Kentucky from 1966 to 1970, he moved to the Center for Man and Environment at Prescott College in 1970. Doybns has observed Papago participation in the Magdalena pilgrimage since 1949.